W9-BLL-564

HILDE AND ELI
Children of the Holocaust

by David A. Adler

illustrated by Karen Ritz

Holiday House / New York

Library of Congress Cataloging-in-Publication Data
Adler, David A.
Hilde and Eli, children of the Holocaust / David A. Adler ;
illustrated by Karen Ritz. — 1st ed.
p.   cm.
ISBN 0-8234-1091-9
1. Holocaust, Jewish (1939–1945)—Biography—Juvenile literature.
2. Jewish children—Biography—Juvenile literature. 3. Rosenzweig,
Hilde, 1923–1941—Juvenile literature. 4. Lax, Eli, 1932–1944—
Juvenile literature. [1. Holocaust, Jewish (1939–1945)—
Biography. 2. Jews—Biography. 3. Rosenzweig, Hilde, 1923–1941.
4. Lax, Eli, 1932–1944.] I. Ritz, Karen, ill. II. Title.
D804.3.A34   1994   93-38229   CIP   AC
940.53′18—dc20

Among the millions of people who died in the Holocaust were two Jewish children, Hilde Rosenzweig and Eli Lax.

Hilde Rosenzweig was a pretty girl with light brown hair and gray eyes. She was born in Frankfurt am Main, Germany on July 4, 1923. Hilde and her older brother Julius lived with their parents, Abraham and Berta Rosenzweig, in an apartment at 27 Fried-bergerland Strasse. The apartment was over a bicycle shop and a bookstore.

The year Hilde was born, 1923, was a difficult year for Germany. Prices went up so fast that no one wanted to hold onto German money. Many people lost their jobs. In November 1923 a little-known politician, Adolf Hitler, led a revolt that failed. Hitler and several of his officers were arrested and jailed.

Hilde was too young to worry about prices and politicians. She liked to ride her tricycle in the park across the street from her apartment.

When Hilde was old enough to go on errands with Julius, they often stopped at Kauf-haus Hansa, a nearby department store. Hilde enjoyed looking at the toys, especially the dolls, dollhouses, and stuffed animals. She dreamed of what she might get for her birth-day or Hanukkah.

Sometimes Hilde's school friends came to visit. They jumped rope and played hop-scotch outside. Inside the apartment they played Ping-Pong on the dining room table.

Until 1932 it seemed to Hilde that her carefree days of school, walks in the park, and visits with friends would go on forever.

But then her father had to close his linen store. Millions of people in Germany had lost their jobs, and in Frankfurt people could no longer afford to buy new sheets, pillowcases, and bedding. Abraham Rosenzweig took work whenever he could get it. He also rented Hilde's bedroom to Mr. and Mrs. Schulherr. Hilde moved into her parents' room.

The Schulherrs were German Protestants. Mrs. Schulherr was a hairdresser and not friendly, but her husband was nice. Sometimes he helped Hilde and Julius with their homework.

By 1932 Adolf Hitler, the politician who was arrested in 1923, was well-known. In 1924, after only nine months in jail, he was released. Since then he had been speaking on street corners and in beer halls about all that was wrong with Germany. These were hard times and people were beginning to listen.

Hitler promised more jobs, greater profits, a stronger army, and extra *Lebensraum*— living space for the German people. And he said the Jews were to blame for all of Germany's problems.

In the 1932 elections, Hitler and his Nazi party received more votes than any other political party. On January 30, 1933, Hitler was named reich chancellor, the prime minister of Germany.

Among the Nazis were uniformed party members, the brown-shirted SA and the black-shirted SS. After Hitler was named chancellor, the Nazis celebrated by attacking and arresting Jews. In March the first concentration camp, a prison for people the Nazis considered their enemies, was opened in Dachau, Germany.

Sometimes, on Friedbergerland Strasse, the Nazis parked vans with loudspeakers blaring Hitler's speeches. But Hilde didn't listen. She didn't hear Hitler shout his hatred of the Jews.

Beginning in March, Hilde saw many DON'T BUY FROM JEWS signs. On Saturday, April 1, 1933, the SA stood in front of Jewish-owned stores to keep people out. That day Hilde stayed away from the shopping area.

It seemed to Hilde that JEWS NOT WANTED signs were being posted everywhere. She felt scared and unwelcome in her own country.

On May 10, 1933, books written by Jews were thrown into the streets and burned.

Some Jews left Germany, but many, including the Rosenzweigs, waited. They expected this wave of hatred to end.

In 1935 laws were passed declaring that Jews were no longer citizens of Germany. They were not even allowed to fly a German flag. Jews were fired from their jobs. Many were forced to sell their property and businesses.

Berta Rosenzweig told her children, Julius and Hilde, to be careful and not upset any non-Jews. The children no longer went outside after nightfall.

In 1938 the Schulherrs moved out of Hilde's bedroom. Mr. Schulherr had taken a job with the Nazis. Of course he could no longer live with Jews.

Julius Rosenzweig knew he had to leave Germany. He applied for a visa to go to the United States. A few months later Hilde and her mother applied for visas, too. Mr. Rosenzweig didn't apply. He had diabetes and was too sick to travel.

Julius's name was placed at the end of a long waiting list. A few months later, when Hilde and her mother applied, their names were placed at the end of the list, too, which by then was even longer.

On March 13, 1938, the German army marched into Austria, a neighboring German-speaking country. Hitler declared it part of Germany.

Eight months later, on November 9, 1938, Hilde witnessed a night of terror. There was shouting outside the apartment and fires throughout the city. The SA, SS, and others were looting Jewish-owned stores and homes. Synagogues were being burned.

Boerne Platze Synagogue, where Hilde and her family prayed, was destroyed. The front window of Kaufhaus Hansa, the store with the dolls and dollhouses of Hilde's long-forgotten dreams, was smashed. The store was looted. Hilde never went to either place again.

Two uniformed Nazis entered the Rosenzweigs' apartment building. They went from one apartment to the next and arrested Jewish men and boys and sent them to concentration camps. Mr. Rosenzweig was sick, so the soldiers didn't take him, and Julius escaped. Before the Nazis came to the Rosenzweig apartment, he had gone out the back way.

The next morning streets in Germany and Austria were littered with ashes and glass.
November 9, 1938, became known as *Kristallnacht,* The Night of Broken Glass.

Julius was able to get a temporary visa for England. He would wait there for his chance to go to the United States. On June 13, 1939, Hilde went with Julius to the train station to say good-bye.

Six days later, on June 19, 1939, Abraham Rosenzweig died. Now only Hilde and her mother remained in the apartment on Friedbergerland Strasse.

Eli Lax never met Hilde Rosenzweig. They lived hundreds of miles apart. But he, too, suffered from the Nazis' hatred of the Jews.

Eli Lax lived with his family in Zarich, a village in the Carpathian Mountains in what was then Czechoslovakia. Eli was the youngest of six children. He was born in 1932.

Eli had no real toys, but he was a happy child who was always smiling. He played with walnuts that fell from the tree in front of his house. He also played with buttons and seeds. Eli loved animals. His family had a cow, chickens, and geese. Eli's brother kept one of the chickens as a pet. Eli helped take care of the animals. He found frogs in the river near his house and took care of them, too.

Eli's father was a rabbi and a teacher. He told his children that school and learning were important.

When Eli was three years old, he went to a religious school. When he was six he went to another school, too, to learn to read and write. He also studied arithmetic, history, and science there. He was at one school or the other thirteen hours a day, from five each morning until six at night. Eli was a good student.

In 1935 Eli's mother died. The next year his oldest sister, Celia, moved to the United States.

Celia sent home a picture postcard of the S.S. *Normandie,* the passenger ship on which she sailed to America. Eli looked at the postcard often. Eli's father told him and the other children that they would be moving to the United States, too. Eli looked forward to having the bicycle he was sure Celia would buy for him.

Celia filled out the necessary papers for her family to move to the United States. Now they only had to wait for the officials at immigration to say they could come.

In September 1938 the Germans took over the Sudetenland, the German-speaking section of Czechoslovakia. Six months later, in March 1939, German troops occupied what was left of Czechoslovakia. Eli and his family were under Nazi rule. Then, on September 1, 1939, the German army invaded Poland. The Second World War began.

At first the Nazis planned to get the Jews out of Germany. Then, with the war, the Nazis devised their "Final Solution." They planned to kill every Jew in Europe.

The German army advanced across Europe, into Poland, Denmark, Norway, Holland, Belgium, France, Greece, Yugoslavia, and the Soviet Union. Among their allies in Europe were Romania, Hungary, Italy, and Bulgaria. In countries ruled by Germany, the Nazis forced Jews to move from villages and towns to large cities near railroad lines. There they were crowded into closed-in sections of the cities called ghettos.

One night, in July 1941, Eli's cousins in Zarich were taken away. Eli heard the screams. After that, Eli was too frightened to sleep at night.

Jews under Nazi rule were desperate to leave, but for most of them there was no place to go. While Julius Rosenzweig was in England, he tried to get visas for Hilde and his mother, but he couldn't.

Beginning in September 1941, Hilde wore on her clothing a yellow star with *Jude*— Jew—printed in the center of it. All Jews in Germany were ordered to wear the star.

In November 1941 the SA came to 27 Friedbergerland Strasse. They forced Hilde and her mother onto a freight train crowded with other Jews. Their car was locked from the outside. They were being taken to the ghetto in Riga, Latvia. On the way the train stopped. The SS filled the freight car with poisonous gas. Everyone inside was killed.

A Jew from Poland came to Zarich to hide from the Nazis. He told Eli and his family what was happening.

Eli's father considered escaping with his children, but there was no place to go. The Nazis were everywhere. Jews from Poland were hiding in Zarich, so he reasoned it must be as safe a place as any to wait for the war to end.

In April 1944 police with rifles forced Eli and his family onto a horse-drawn wagon to a ghetto in Irshava, two miles away. Four families, more than twenty people, were crowded into one room.

In May, Eli and his family were chased with clubs onto a train. They rode in a locked freight car for two hours until they came to the Munkács ghetto.

Eli was scared, but he still had hope. He spoke to his sisters about going to America.

After three weeks in Munkács, Eli and his family were pulled out of the apartment. The Nazis swung their clubs and yelled, "*Schnell! Schnell!*—Fast! Fast!" Eli's sisters held him as they ran to the train.

There were more than one hundred people in the locked cattle car. Some of them were sick. Many were crying.

The train stopped after three days. They were at Auschwitz, a concentration camp in Poland. The car doors were opened by Nazis with guns and guard dogs. Eli held his father's hand. They got off the train and stood in line on the platform. A Nazi officer directed some people one way and some another. Eli, his father, and his brother were sent to the left. Eli's sisters were sent to the right.

The Nazis told Eli, his brother, father, and the others that they needed showers. They were told to undress, fold their clothes, and remember where they put them. Then they were led into what looked like a large bathhouse. The doors were locked. Poison pellets were dropped in through an opening in the ceiling. Eli, his brother, and father and all the others in the "bathhouse" were killed. Later their bodies were burned.

Jews were shot, gassed, and tortured. By May 8, 1945, the day the war in Europe ended, some six million Jews had been murdered by the Nazis. One and a half million of them were children. Among those killed were Hilde Rosenzweig and Eli Lax.

Author's Note

The Nazis did not persecute only Jews. They also killed Romanies, Serbs, Jehovah's Witnesses, homosexuals, Communists, the elderly, the handicapped, the mentally ill, beggars, and Russian prisoners of war. But the subject of this book, the "Holocaust," which literally means a huge destruction by fire, refers to the murder of Jews by the Nazis.

The information included here about Hilde Rosenzweig and her family was given to me by her brother Julius. He came to the United States in 1940 and served in the United States Army from 1943–1946. The photograph on the previous page, of fifteen-year-old Hilde in 1938, was in an album Julius took with him when he went to England. Of Hilde's more than forty first cousins in Germany and Poland, only thirteen survived the Holocaust.

The information included here about Eli Lax and his family was given to me by his sisters, Eve Slomovits, Lilly Friedman, and Ilona Traeger. They were taken to Auschwitz with Eli, their brother Michael, and their father. When they arrived and Eli was sent to the left, they were sent to the right with the group selected for slave labor. During the next year, until they were liberated on April 15, 1945, they were moved to five other concentration camps. The sisters feel they survived because they were somehow able to stay together. The photograph on the previous page was taken in 1940 when Eli was eight. It was sent to Celia in the United States. It's the only photograph the sisters have of Eli. Eli's father was one of twelve children. His mother was one of six. Eli had more than one hundred first cousins. About thirty survived the Holocaust.

—David A. Adler